These giant animals lived in **ancient** Australia. They are called megafauna. Many megafauna lived in Australia about 1.6 million years ago.

Fossil Remains

We know that megafauna lived in Australia because their **fossils** have been found. Many fossils have been found in caves and dried lakes.

Paleontologists at work on a megafauna fossil.

The Giants of Ancient Australia

Dianne Irving
Rob Kiely

Contents

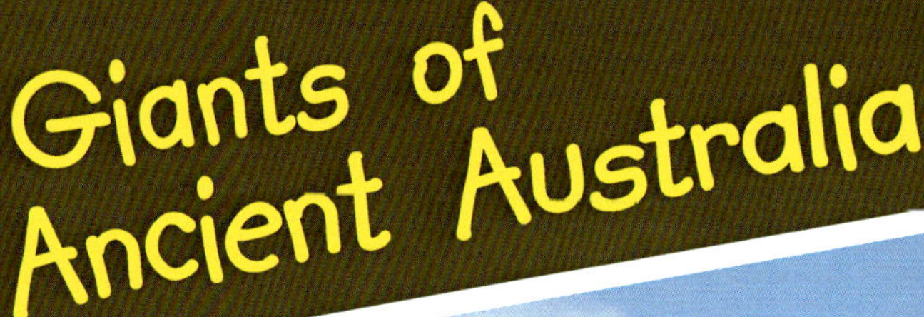

Giants of Ancient Australia

What if you saw:

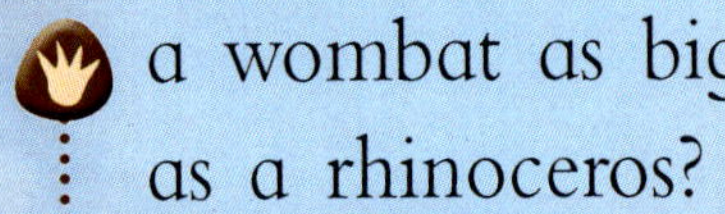

- a wombat as big as a rhinoceros?

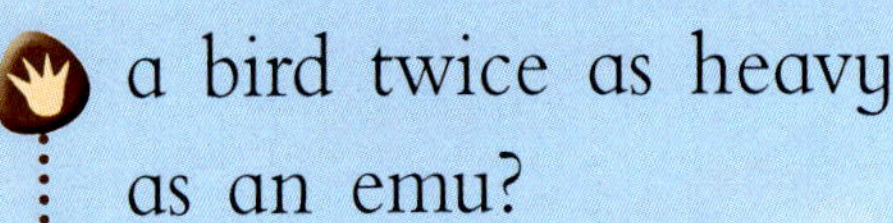

- a bird twice as heavy as an emu?

- a lizard as heavy as a polar bear?

What would you think?

Scientists study these fossils to find out how and when these animals lived. Scientists try to put megafauna skeletons back together or make models. This helps them learn what the animals may have looked like.

A paleontologist at work on an ancient marine reptile fossil.

Paleontologists are scientists who dig up and study fossils.

Diprotodon

Diprotodon:
say *di-pro-toe-don*

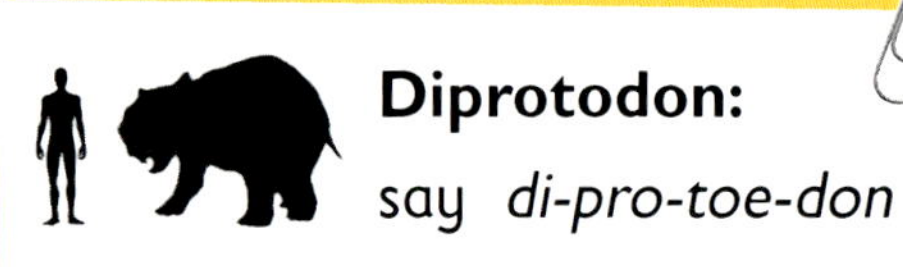

This giant megafauna was the largest **marsupial** to have ever lived. It was about the same size as a rhinoceros.

Diprotodon was a plant eater. It had two large front teeth, like a wombat, to help it eat woody plants.

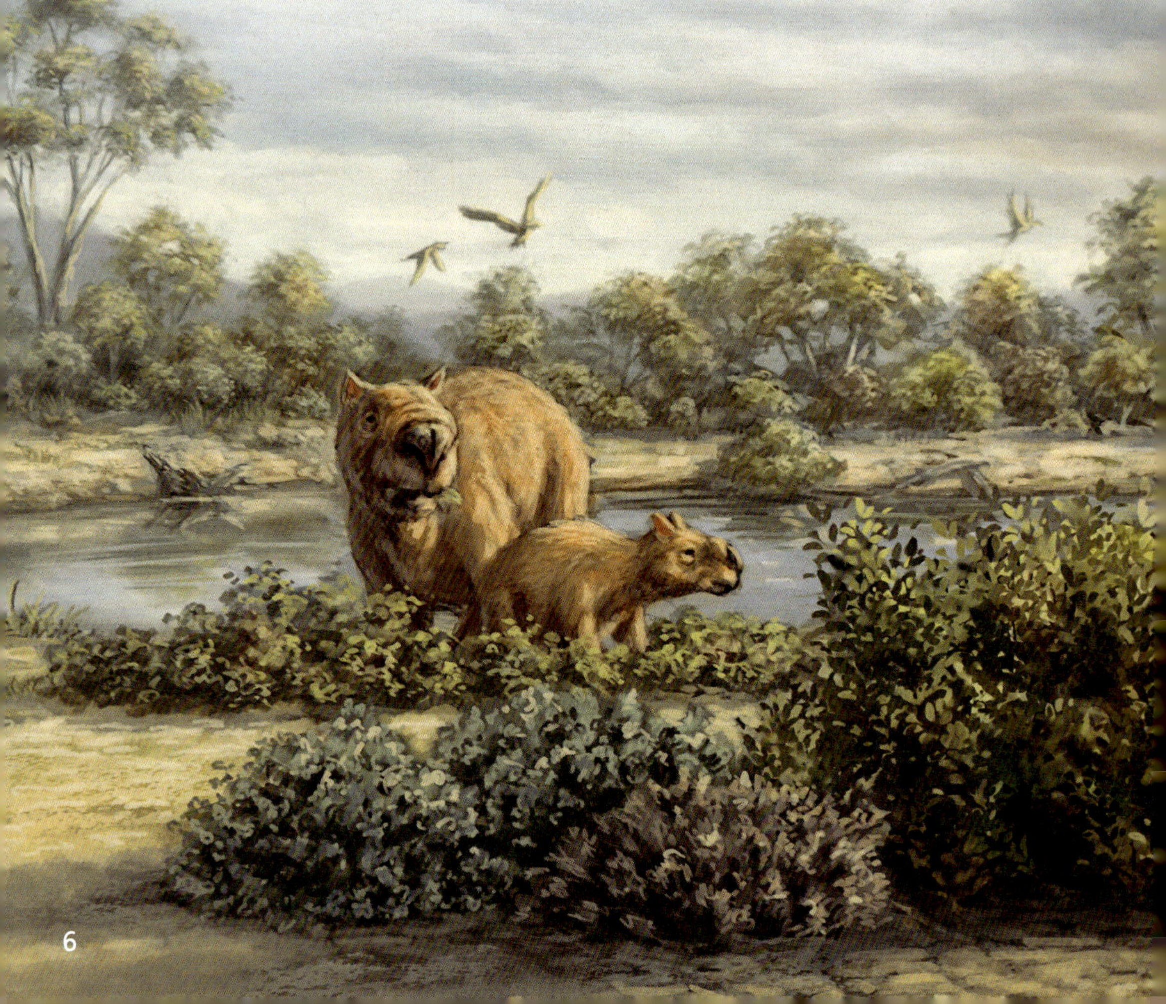

Predators of Diprotodon were the Tasmanian Tiger, mega-crocodiles and marsupial lions.

Diprotodon could weigh up to 2 tonnes. It was 3 metres long and almost 2 metres high at the shoulder.

Giant Short-faced Kangaroo

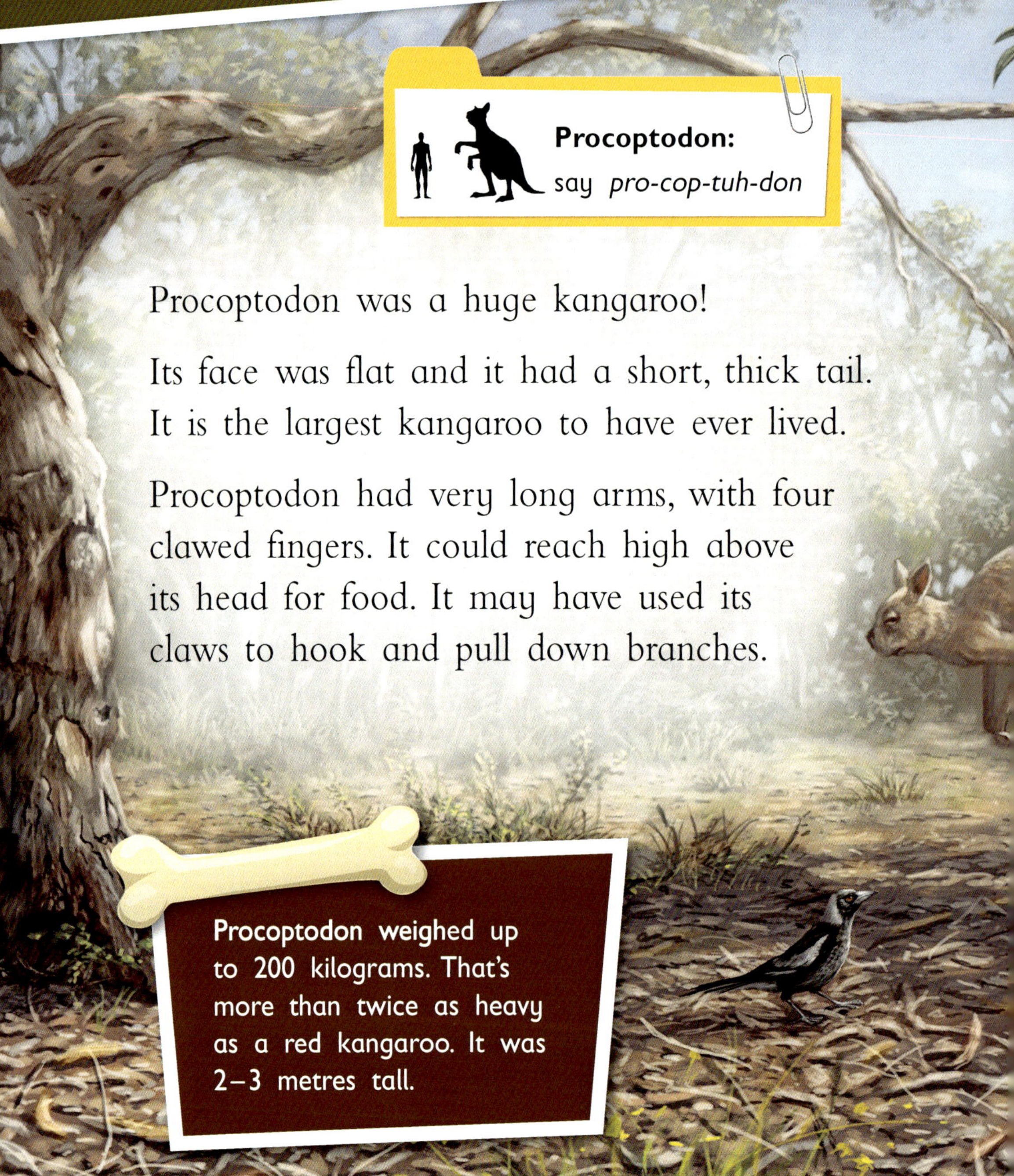

Procoptodon:
say *pro-cop-tuh-don*

Procoptodon was a huge kangaroo!

Its face was flat and it had a short, thick tail. It is the largest kangaroo to have ever lived.

Procoptodon had very long arms, with four clawed fingers. It could reach high above its head for food. It may have used its claws to hook and pull down branches.

Procoptodon weighed up to 200 kilograms. That's more than twice as heavy as a red kangaroo. It was 2–3 metres tall.

Giant Goanna

Megalania:

say *meg-ar-lane-ee-ar*

From the Megalania bones found, we know that this giant goanna was the largest land lizard that ever lived.

Megalania means "ancient great roamer". It lived in open forest and woodland. It was a meat eater and had sharp, ridged teeth – like steak knives!

Megalania could grow up to 7 metres long and weighed 600 kilograms. That's twice as big as today's Komodo dragon.

Thunder Bird

Genyornis:
say *jen-ee-or-nis*

Genyornis was a large flightless bird. It belonged to an animal family called thunder birds. It looked a bit like an emu and had clawed toes and tiny wings.

Genyornis means "jaw bird". Genyornis had a large beak, but no teeth. It ate leaves and twigs and may also have eaten small animals. It swallowed pebbles to help break down its food.

The Genyornis was about 2 metres tall and weighed up to 250 kilograms.

Marsupial Lion

Thylacoleo is the largest meat-eating **mammal** to have lived in Australia. It got its name because it looked a bit like a big cat.

It had strong front legs and a big skull. Its strong jaws and sharp teeth made it a powerful predator.

Thylacoleo was about 1.5 metres long and weighed up to 120 kilograms.

Giant Echidna

Zaglossus:
say *zag-loss-us*

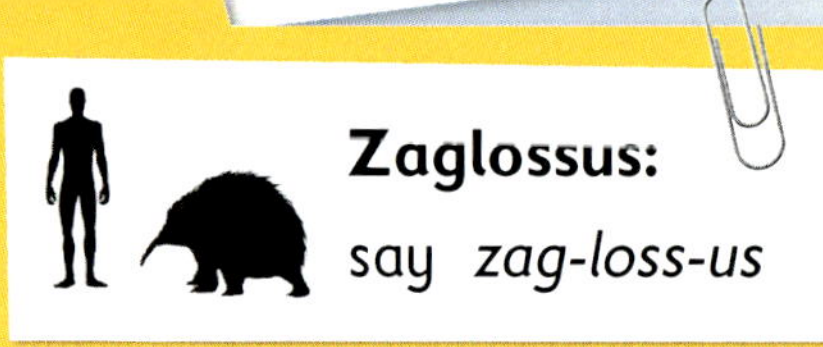

Only a few Zaglossus bones have been found. Scientists think it was about one metre long. That's about three times the size of an echidna today.

Like today's echidnas, the Zaglossus fed on worms, ants and beetles. It had a long **snout**. Short but strong legs helped with digging. When it was in danger, it could roll up in a ball to protect itself.

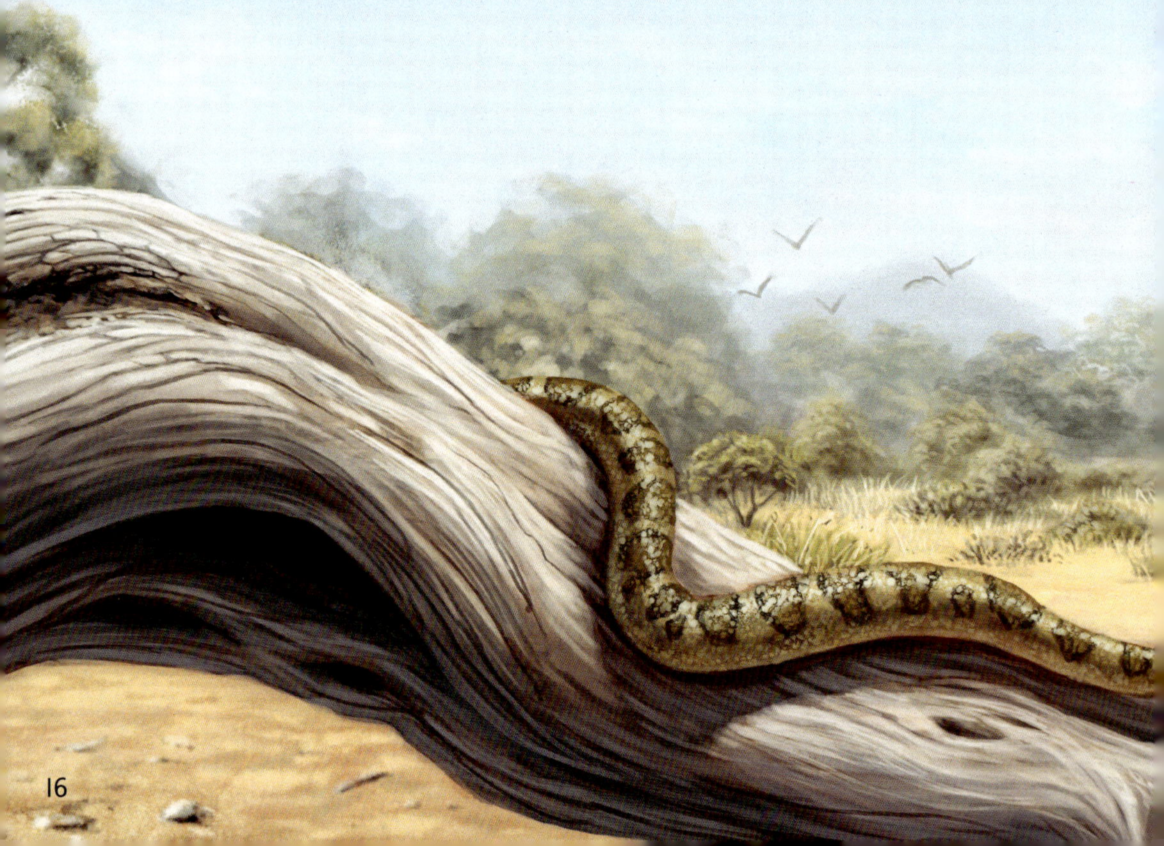

Zaglossus was the biggest **monotreme** ever to have lived.

Tasmanian Tiger

Thylacine:
say *thy-la-seen*

The Thylacine got the name Tasmanian Tiger because of its striped coat and yellow fur. It had 15 to 20 brown stripes on its back. It was once found all over Australia but it became **extinct** in 1936.

Thylacines grew to be about one metre long. They were meat eaters, hunting wallabies and other small animals.

Mega-crocodile

Quinkana:
say *qwin-kana*

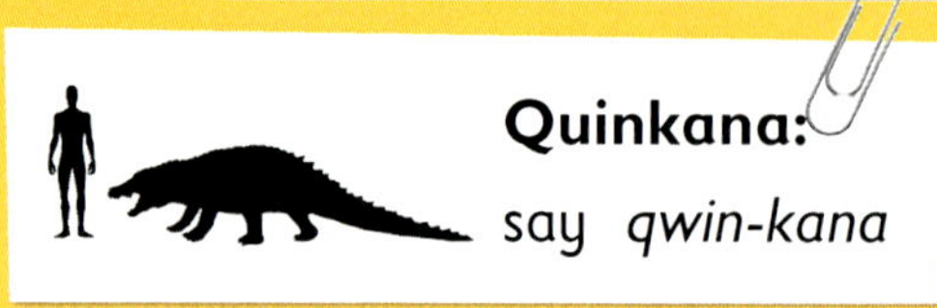

This animal was a mega-crocodile! But it did not live in water like crocodiles today. It lived on land.

The Quinkana had long legs and could move very fast. It ate mammals, birds and other **reptiles**. Like Megalania, this reptile had very sharp cutting teeth for eating its **prey**.

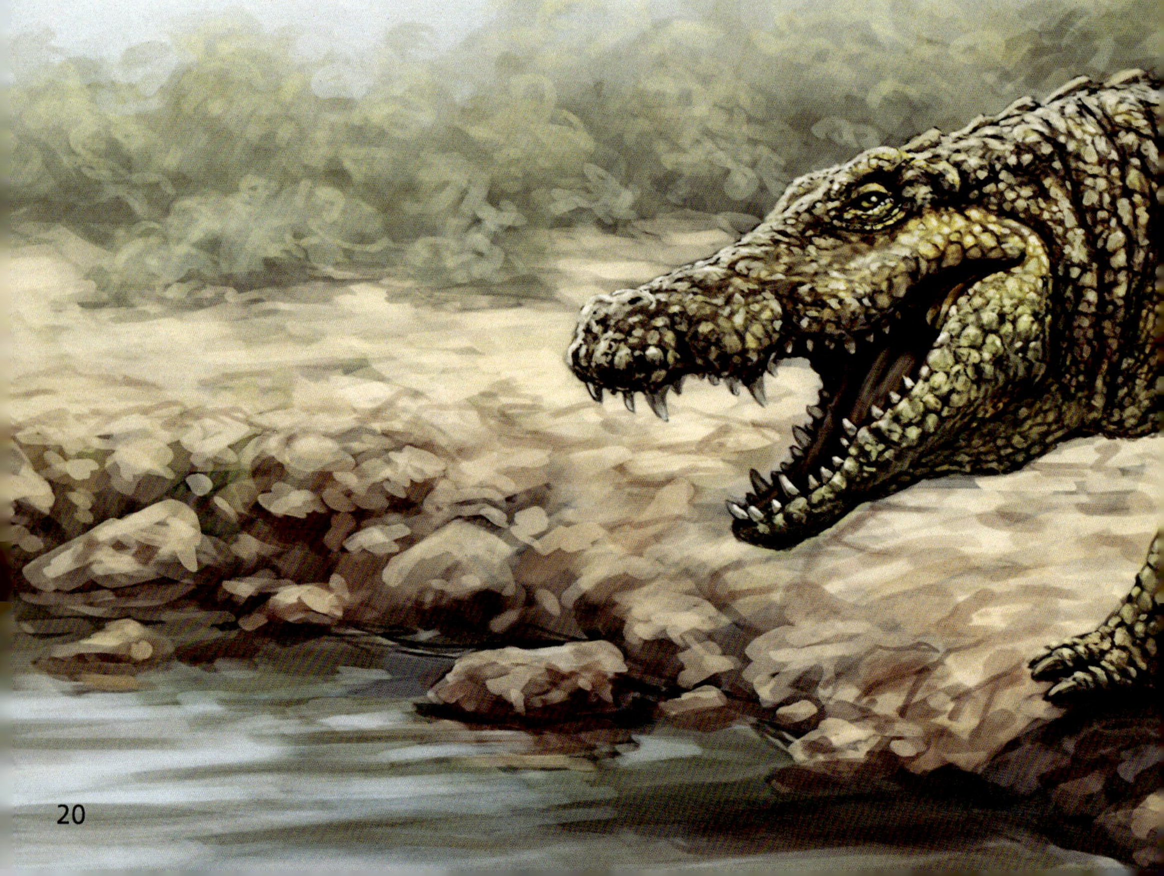

This ancient crocodile grew up to 7 metres long.

Marsupial Tapir

Palorchestes:
say *pal-or-kess-tes*

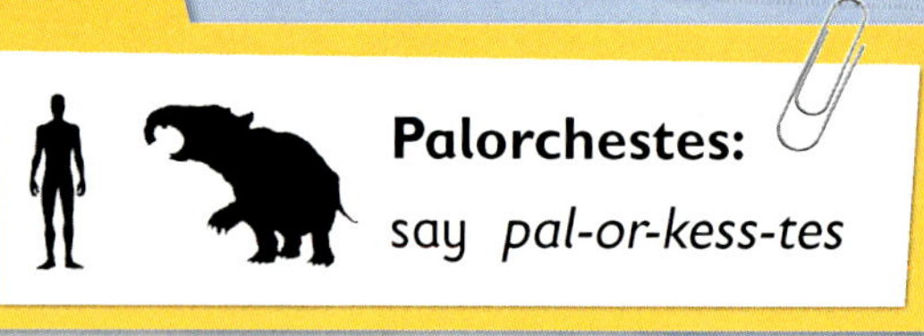

Palorchestes was the size of a cow.

It had a strange looking head with a long nose that looked a bit like a trunk.

This mammal was a plant eater. It had strong front legs and sharp claws. It used these to **tear** bark and rip up roots to eat.

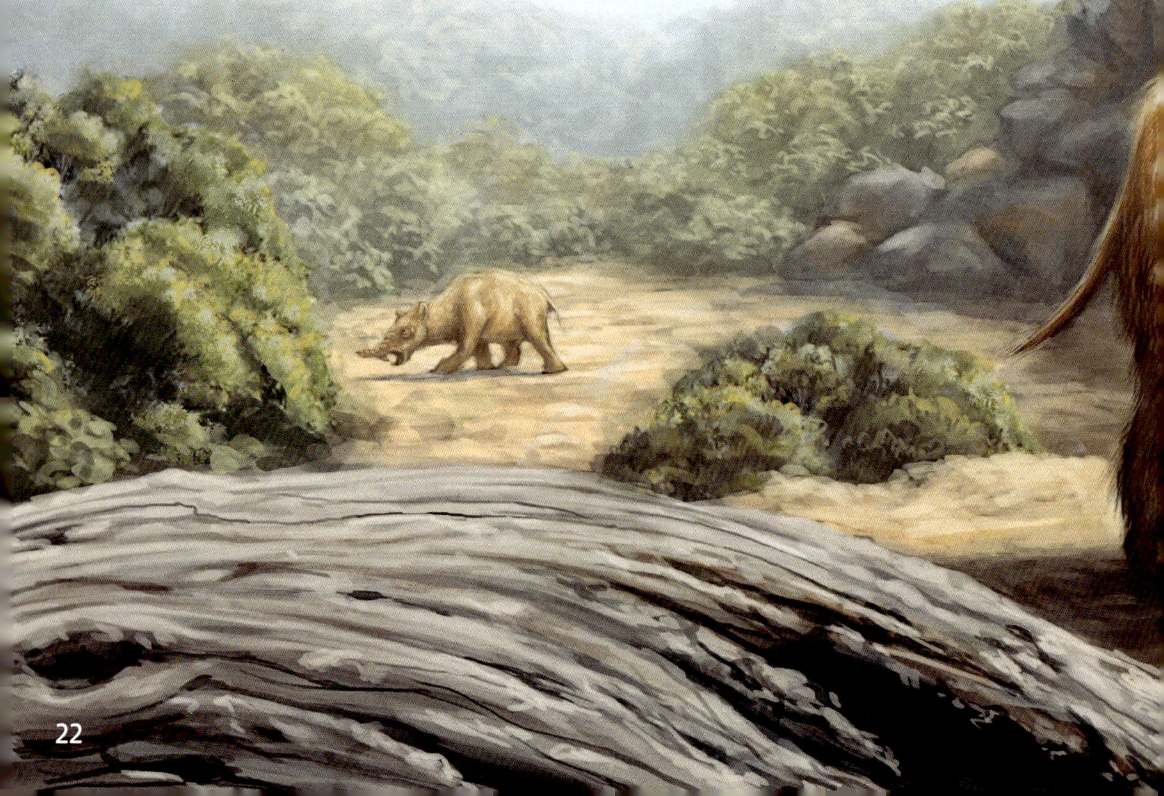

These animals are thought to have weighed about 500 kilograms and to have been about 2 metres long.

Zygomaturus

Zygomaturus:
say *zy-go-ma-chur-us*

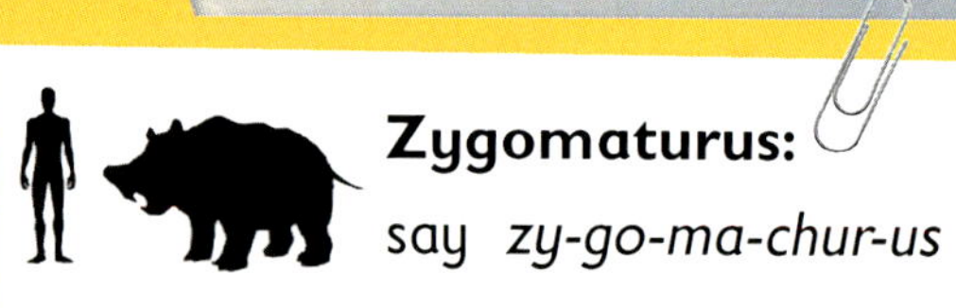

Zygomaturus was a giant marsupial that looked a bit like a hippo. It ate reeds and other grassy **herbs** that grew near water. It scooped up its food using its two bottom front teeth that were like forks.

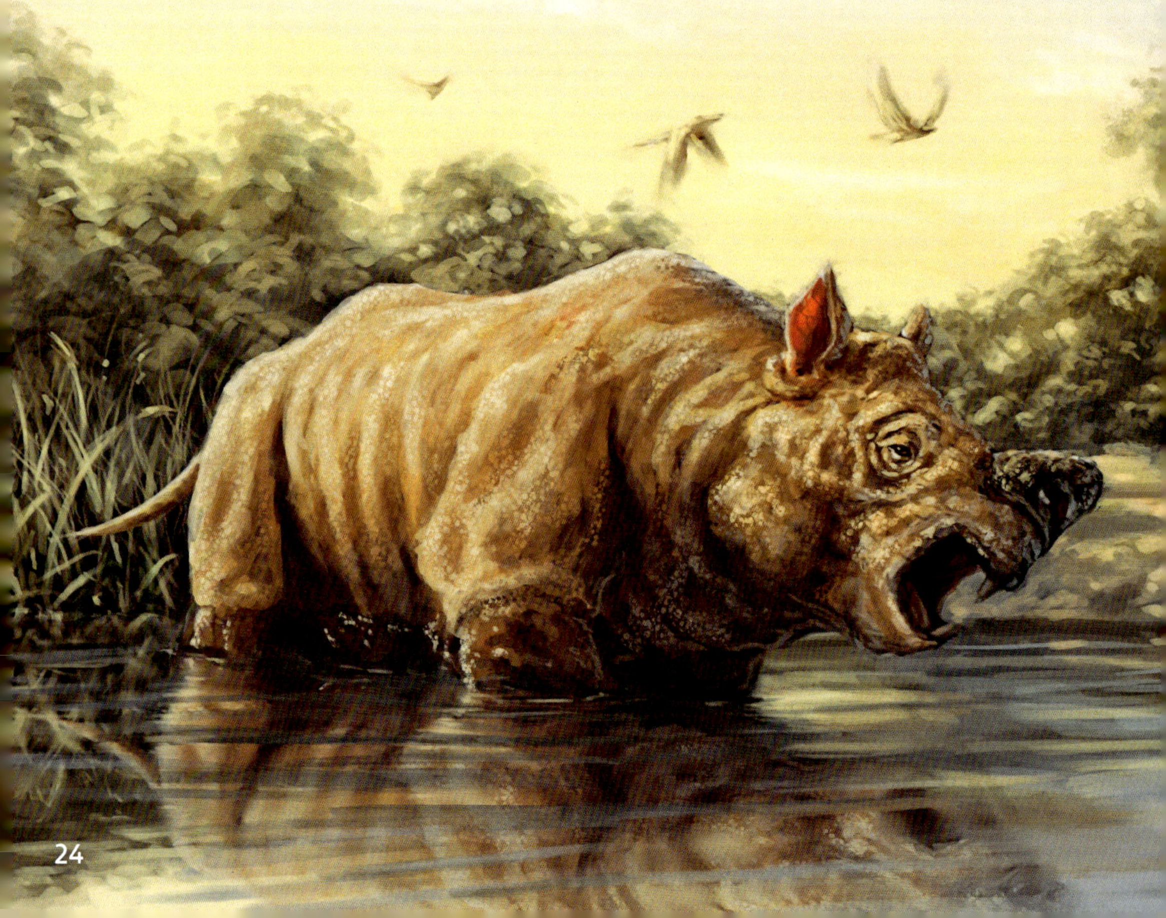

Zygomaturus was about 2.5 metres long and one metre high at the shoulder. It weighed 300–500 kilograms.

Megafauna Timeline

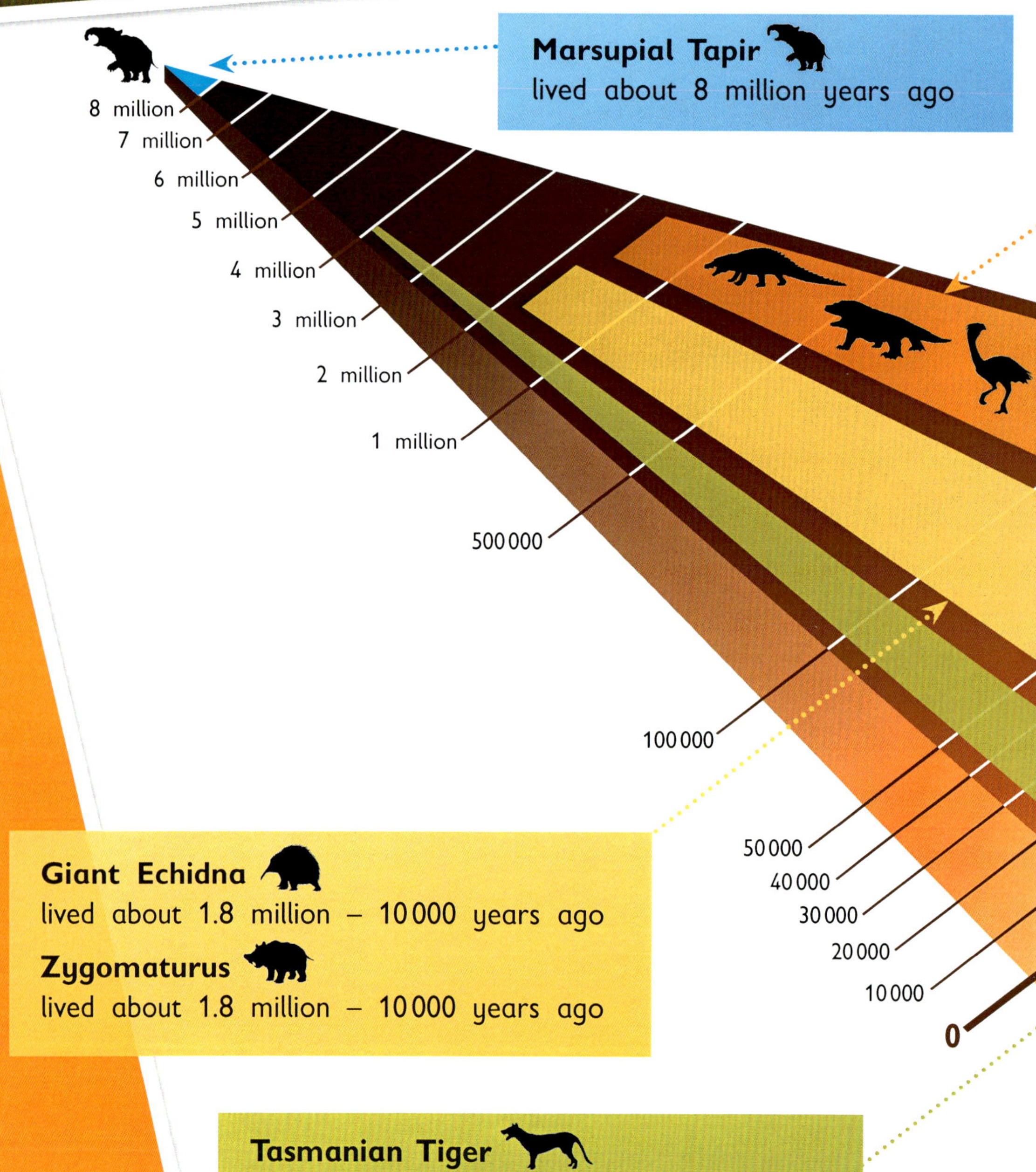

Marsupial Tapir
lived about 8 million years ago

Giant Echidna
lived about 1.8 million – 10 000 years ago

Zygomaturus
lived about 1.8 million – 10 000 years ago

Tasmanian Tiger
lived about 4 million years ago – 1936

Diprotodon	lived about 1.6 million – 40 000 years ago
Giant Kangaroo	lived about 1.6 million – 40 000 years ago
Giant Goanna	lived about 1.6 million – 40 000 years ago
Thunder Bird	lived about 1.6 million – 40 000 years ago
Mega-crocodile	lived about 1.6 million – 40 000 years ago
Marsupial Lion	lived about 1.6 million – 40 000 years ago

40 000 years ago

10 000 years ago

1936

TODAY

1000

1500

1600

1700

1800

1900

2000

Extinction

Scientists think most megafauna became extinct about 40–50 000 years ago. There are different ideas about why they became extinct.

Climate

It may be because of changes in the climate. The climate kept changing from cool to warm. It was often very dry. Plants changed too, and animals may have run out of food.

Humans

It may be because they were hunted by humans. Most megafauna were slow-moving and easy to kill.

It may have been because humans used fires in hunting. This changed the animals' environment.

Scientists have found stone tools that might have been used by early humans for cutting up megafauna. Ancient animal bones have been found with chips and cuts on them that look like tool marks.

The Future of Fossils

Finding new fossil sites means there is always something more for scientists to learn about megafauna.

This giant crocodile ruled the swamps 100 million years ago.

There are also new ways of telling how old fossils are. Scientists can make new discoveries about megafauna and how they lived and died. Their fossil finds may end up in a **museum** for all of us to see.

Glossary

ancient	very old; belonging to times long ago
extinct	when a type of animal or plant dies out
fossils	the remains of animals or plants from long ago
herbs	leafy green plants, usually with a strong smell
mammal	a warm-blooded animal that feeds its young milk
marsupial	a mammal with a pouch for its young
monotreme	a mammal that lays eggs
museum	a building that keeps interesting and old collections
predators	animals that hunt and eat other animals
prey	animals hunted for food
reptiles	cold-blooded animals that have scales
snout	the front part of an animal's face, with nose, mouth and jaw
tear	rip apart

Index